TEEN LIFE™

FREQUENTLY ASKED QUESTIONS ABOUT

Suicide

Sandra
Giddens

ROSEN
PUBLISHING®

New York

Published in 2009 by The Rosen Publishing Group, Inc.
29 East 21st Street, New York, NY 10010

First Edition

Library of Congress Cataloging-in-Publication Data

Giddens, Sandra.
Frequently asked questions about suicide / Sandra Giddens.
    p. cm.—(FAQ: teen life)
ISBN-13: 978-1-4042-1811-6 (library binding)
1. Suicide. 2. Teenagers—Suicidal behavior. I. Title.
HV6545.G545 2009
616.85'8445—dc22

2008000747

Manufactured in the United States of America
CPSIA Compliance Information: Batch #LR014010YA: For Further Information Contact Rosen Publishing, New York, New York at 1-800-237-9932

Contents

Chapter one

HOW SERIOUS IS SUICIDE?

When someone says the word "suicide," it is usually met with silence. Just say the word, and immediately people want to avoid talking about the subject. Suicide describes the voluntary and intentional act of taking one's own life. It comes from two Latin root words, *sui* (of oneself) and *cidium* (a killing or slaying). It is very difficult to understand an act that is contrary to living one's day-to-day life. Most people want to experience aging, not to end their life prematurely.

Unfortunately, people are not transparent; you cannot look into their heads to see what they are thinking or feeling. Most people go through their day looking at people but not really seeing individuals. They might not notice that what they are seeing could be the person's cry for help. Is it the person who comes from the perfect family but feels that he or she does not measure up? Or is it someone who comes from an abusive

Even remotely contemplating suicide is a serious issue. Make sure you talk to someone even if you're having so-called "harmless thoughts."

family? Do you connect with the person who is always eating alone? Do you see the person begging for help but not voicing it? Connecting with people could be the first step in suicide prevention.

If you are a teenager contemplating suicide, you may want to talk openly about your thoughts, but you may think society seems unwilling to hear them. You may start feeling isolated and in emotional pain and may begin to feel more and more alone. If you could have the opportunity to talk openly about your feelings, you may finally feel understood. By not keeping suicide under lock and key and trying to understand its occurrence, there could possibly be a means of preventing it from happening to you or someone you know.

Current State of Suicide

The act of taking one's life has occurred throughout history. Even today, news stories tell of people taking their own lives.

When celebrities, such as rock star Kurt Cobain, commit suicide, they regretfully inspire others to do the same.

Young suicide bombers give up their lives for what they see as noble causes. Suicide continues to be a major concern in today's society, and the problem is not lessening or going away.

You probably have heard of or know friends, family members, famous stars, or acquaintances who have ended their lives through the act of suicide. Suicide is the eighth leading cause of death in the United States. It is estimated that five million people now living in the United States have attempted suicide. The World Health Organization (WHO) estimates that the suicide rate worldwide could rise to 1.5 million suicides per year by the year 2020. Dr. Catherine Le Galès-Camus of WHO says, "Suicide is a tragic global public health problem. Worldwide, more people die from suicide than from all homicides and wars combined."

Teen Suicide Statistics

It is very frightening when you look at suicide statistics for young men and women. Look at the face of a clock and start counting. Approximately once every eighty seconds a teenager attempts to take his or her own life, and approximately once every one hundred minutes a teen actually completes a suicide. After car accidents and murder, suicide is the third leading cause of death for fifteen- to twenty-four-year-olds in the United States.

Suicide rates among ten- to fourteen-year-olds have nearly doubled in the past few decades. White teenage boys have the highest rate of suicide. Black teenagers are now more than twice as likely to kill themselves as they were twenty years ago. Out of every five people who take their own lives, four are likely to be male. Females are three times more likely to attempt suicide, but males are the ones who complete their attempts. Males tend to use more violent methods, like shooting themselves, than women do. Women might use pills, so, therefore, some can be saved. Recently, many teenage girls who have died by suicide have used violent methods like guns. Gun deaths continue to be on a steady climb. Frighteningly, nearly 60 percent of all suicides in the United States are completed with a gun.

The suicide rate for teen girls has skyrocketed recently, shocking and puzzling experts. Suicide rates among fifteen- to nineteen-year-old girls have risen 32 percent, based on the most recent data available in 2007. (This data shows the differences between 2003 and 2004.) Rates for males in that age group rose, too, but only by 9 percent. And the suicide rate

There can be many reasons that young people commit suicide, such as depression, bad grades, and troubles at home.

for preteen and young teen girls, aged ten to fourteen, jumped a staggering 76 percent. Experts are scrambling for answers and asking themselves, Why has this happened?

The rate of suicide for teens may even be higher than reported. Automobile crashes account for the leading cause of death for fifteen- to nineteen-year-olds. Law enforcement officials might look at a car crash of a single teenage driver, see no skid marks, and put down the cause as "accident." In fact, these car crashes could be "autocides," the term for suicide by car crash.

The transition into adulthood can be difficult. As an adolescent, you are a part of a particularly vulnerable group that can encounter pressure from your family and peer groups. Some problems you may face include family breakdown, sexuality, body image (anorexia, bulimia, obesity), and social, school, and peer pressures. These problems could lead to a state of depression, which is the most common cause of suicide.

two

WHAT ARE THE RISK FACTORS?

How you deal with stress affects your emotional state. If you aren't able to cope in healthy ways, you may be putting yourself at a higher risk for suicide. If you're feeling depressed, it's easy for you to fall into reckless behavior. You might find that you put yourself in risky situations that make life even more difficult to handle. Risk factors are circumstances that may put a depressed person at a higher risk of suicide. It is important to know that not all risk factors lead to suicide. Some of the main risk factors include:

- Gambling
- Alcohol and drug abuse
- School and/or personal crisis
- Setting high standards for oneself
- Legal problems
- Social isolation

Addictions play a major role in influencing suicide. Not only are many drugs, such as alcohol, depressants, addicts may also feel that they have no chance of quitting.

- ➤ Trouble at home
- ➤ Bullying victim
- ➤ Unplanned pregnancy
- ➤ Previous suicide attempt
- ➤ Depression
- ➤ Media influence and cluster suicides (copycat suicides)
- ➤ New situations like beginning college
- ➤ Chemical imbalances
- ➤ Early traumas
- ➤ Sexual identity issues

Gamblers have the highest suicide rate of any group of people who have an addiction, whether it's drugs or behavioral addiction. Although they can't gamble legally, teens can easily find a way by going to casinos and gambling Web sites, using campus bookies to bet on sports games, and betting on cards at school. Presently, poker is the new rage among teens. Many teens stay up all night online or attend parties where gambling is the main focus. Teens see gambling as a way to make a quick buck; what they cannot envision is the cycle of losing and going into debt. Many teens who constantly play on the Internet, sometimes winning and many times losing, are isolated. They start craving the thrill of the win and of course get despondent, or let down, at the loss.

Alcohol and Drug Abuse

Teens sometimes turn to drugs and alcohol in an attempt to reduce the pain they are feeling from stress and feelings of helplessness or hopelessness. Teens can start feeling depressed as young as age twelve or thirteen. If you're depressed and you do not seek professional help, you might seek other methods to relieve yourself of your symptoms. You may turn to drugs and alcohol to help you deal with your pain. Keep in mind that teens who engage in high-risk behaviors, such as sex and alcohol and drugs, have significantly higher odds of suicidal thoughts and suicide attempts.

When you first start to drink alcohol, it can elevate your mood, but it is in fact a depressant drug. Having two to three glasses of alcohol can impair your vision, speech, coordination, and sense of balance, and can cause loss of self-control. If you already suffer from depression, alcohol can increase your feelings. If you are feeling suicidal, these feelings may become enhanced after drinking alcohol. The relationship between alcoholism and suicide appears to be stronger among males than females. Studies show that among young people who take their own lives, the drugs most commonly abused after alcohol were marijuana, cocaine, amphetamines, and combinations of these.

Young people who have not been known to have suicidal feelings before may become vulnerable to these emotions under the influence of chemicals, particularly after prolonged use. Autopsies of adolescent suicide victims show that one-third to one-half of teenagers were under the influence of drugs or alcohol before they killed themselves.

Problems at School

School can certainly be stressful for you. There is the stress of passing tests, completing day-to-day homework, getting into a college, being popular, and basically fitting in. There are also the physical, sexual, and emotional changes that occur through adolescence. This is the time for change and discovery. It is also a time for moods to be somewhat erratic. Most of this is quite normal. It is when you feel out of control and in crisis that help is needed.

Some school problems can be attributed to difficulties with academics, perhaps because you have a learning disability. At times, school problems can be a warning sign of deeper issues. It may be a sign that you're feeling depressed.

Many teens feel there is an in crowd and that they are not part of it. If somebody can't make any friends, this can be cause for concern. You and your classmates can look around and identify peers who are loners. They may not want to be that way but have not found a way to break into a crowd, or perhaps they use their aloneness to hide their own insecurities.

Some students who take their own lives are indeed the opposite of the rebellious teen. Setting high standards and not achieving them as well as family pressures of setting overly high expectations to excel can also be problems. These are anxious,

Problems at school can easily trigger suicidal thoughts. You should take comfort in the fact that there's nothing serious enough that warrants taking your own life.

insecure students who have a desperate desire to be liked, to fit in, and to do well. Their expectations are so high that they demand too much of themselves and are condemned to constant disappointment.

Being a teenager is not an easy experience. There are times when you are feeling up and times when you are feeling down. It is when the down times and the negative feelings start to take over that the need to get help and support is crucial.

Bullying and Cyberbullying

Bullying is when someone or a group of people do or say hurtful things so they can ultimately have power over you. Some of the ways you can be bullied is by being called inappropriate names, having negative things said or written about you, being purposefully left out of activities, being ostracized, being threatened, being made to feel uncomfortable or frightened in your school or home life, having your things taken or removed, being physically hit, or being pushed into doing things you do not want to do.

The Internet has created a whole new world of communication and a new method for bullying to occur. Young people gravitate to their computers to talk to friends on instant messaging servers like MSN, make their own personal blogs, or do text messaging on their computers or cell phones. Media Awareness Network research shows that 50 percent of students say they are alone online most of the time. Only about 16 percent say they talk to their parents a lot about what they do online. Because bullies tend to harass their victims away from the watchful eye of an adult, the

With the growing popularity of social networking sites, bullying has found its way onto the Internet. Cyberbullying can be another trigger for suicidal thoughts.

Internet has provided the perfect tool to reach others, bully them, and many times remain anonymous. The frightening part of this is that the home can no longer be a refuge for the victim.

While most interactions online are positive, there are people who use this form of communication in a very negative manner. They antagonize and intimidate people. This has become known as cyberbullying. It is a way to harass, humiliate, or threaten others using the Internet or cell phones. There are cases in which cyberbullying has been one of the main causes for young people to end their lives by committing suicide.

One method of bullying involves taking pictures on cell phones. It operates like this: Someone takes a picture of a peer, then the bully puts the picture on the Internet and either attaches it to different bodies or manipulates the photo of the peer into compromising poses, sometimes pornographic ones. The victim then discovers that he or she is plastered all over the Internet and is humiliated and wants to hide from life.

Another form of bullying is when the person is locked out from everyone's messaging servers. No one will accept him or her. That person feels isolated and degraded. The victim's humiliation can be tragic in the end for all.

Relationship Problems

Around this time in your life, you are starting to feel sexual attraction for others. Maybe your peers or you are romantically involved with somebody. With relationships also come breakups. There have been cases in which teens of both genders have attempted suicide because they could not cope with their romantic breakups. This has been more prevalent among females.

Relationship with Your Parents

The relationship between you and your parents is a significant one. Many researchers trace suicidal feelings and behavior to

Relationship problems often lead to depression, which, in turn, can lead to negative thoughts about your personality, friends, and life in general.

long-term depressive illness rooted in very dysfunctional parent-child relationships.

In a study by the American Academy of Pediatrics, adult women who said they were physically or emotionally abused as children were more likely to have mental problems, to suffer from depression, and to have attempted suicide.

The breakup of the two-parent family, whether from divorce, desertion, or the death of a parent, makes children more vulnerable. Children's advocates still maintain it's the quality of the parenting, not the makeup of the family, that matters most.

Suicidal behavior does not necessarily happen all at once. A family's background and circumstances may predispose the teen to suicidal behavior. The factor of marriage and separation is highly correlated with suicidal behavior. Within families, social, economic, personal, and behavioral factors can cause stress or depression that may predispose members to suicide. Suicidal behavior may run in families.

Depression

Depression is the main cause of suicide. People aged fifteen to twenty-four suffer the highest rate of depression and suicidal thoughts, and yet they are also the least likely to seek outside help of any age group. It is important if you are feeling depressed to seek help and support.

Depression is an internal state. The image people who are depressed project to the rest of the world may not reveal the true desperation they are, in fact, experiencing internally. If you are depressed, you may exhibit a few or a number of the following signs of depression:

- Losing interest in hobbies, school, and friends
- Complaining about a lot of aches and pains
- Feeling blue, rebellious, and angered
- Sleeping too much or too little
- Letting hygiene go
- Low energy
- Crying spells

- Trouble with day-to-day concentration or memory
- Persistent sad, anxious, or empty mood
- Feelings of hopelessness and pessimism
- Feelings of guilt, worthlessness, and helplessness
- Difficulty making decisions
- Weight loss or gain
- Restlessness and irritability
- Persistent symptoms such as headaches, digestive disorders, and chronic pain
- Thoughts of death and suicide
- Suicide attempts

The Blues

There are different forms of depression. A less severe kind of depression is when you feel emotionally down or sad but not for an extended period of time. You may start eating more or less and do not feel really energetic. This is a temporary state, and you usually bounce back again.

Seasonal Affective Disorder

If you have seasonal affective disorder (SAD), you have difficulties adjusting to less sunlight during the winter months and may feel depressed and blue.

Clinical Depression

Clinical depression means that the depression is severe enough to require treatment. If you are clinically depressed, you feel sad most of the day, nearly every day, for at least two weeks. Often,

Sometimes, there are no outside triggers for suicide, just inherent clinical depression. If you're feeling depressed, it's important that you speak to a trusted adult.

you cannot sleep or sleep too much, lose interest in activities that you once enjoyed, lose your sense of value for yourself, and feel worthless and helpless. Because you have a severe loss or increase in appetite, a weight change may start to become noticeable.

chapter three

WHO IS AT RISK?

Each year, more than 30,000 Americans take their own lives. In 2001, 4,234 youths between ten and twenty-four years old committed suicide. Males between fifteen and nineteen were 4.8 times more likely than females to take their own lives in 2001. In that year, American Indians and Alaskan Natives had a suicide rate of 18.8 per 100,000, compared to rates of 11.5 for white youths, 7.3 for African Americans, 6.4 for Asian Americans, and 6.1 for Hispanics youth. Gay teens are more at risk of suicide than their heterosexual counterparts.

Native Canadians and Native Americans

Depression and suicide are huge problems among Native American teens. They have to live in a world where racism is on the rise, and they have to struggle to fit in. The suicide

Suicide statistics show that the Native American population has an extremely high suicide rate compared to other ethnicities.

rates for Native American youth are 1.5 to 3 times higher than that of other ethnicities in the United States, and suicide is the second leading cause of death for Native American youth between the ages of fifteen and twenty-four.

When Native American teens feel there is nowhere to go, some turn to inhaling gasoline, alcohol abuse, and drugs to deal with their depression. Drug and alcohol abuse affect up to 70 percent of the First Nations Canadian tribal population. Suicide occurs roughly five to six times more often among First Nations youth than other youth in Canada. The ratio of young men to young women completing suicide is four to one.

In an attempt to turn the situation around, efforts are continually being made to help these youth help themselves through education, support groups, and treatment facilities and programs.

Black and Latino Teens

Among fifteen- to nineteen-year-old black males, suicide rates from 1980 to 2001 have increased 80 percent, or 7.3 per 100,000.

Suicide rates among black and Latino teens has increased in recent years due to a number of factors, including socioeconomic conditions.

Although lower than whites, black youths aged ten to fourteen showed the largest increase in suicide rates, 1.7 per 100,000.

During 1997 to 2001, a total of 8,744 Hispanics died from suicide; 7,439 (85 percent) were males. Approximately 50 percent of all suicides occurred among people aged ten to thirty-four years old.

Black and Latino teens from lower socioeconomic backgrounds reported that they had suicidal thoughts and said they had few adults in their lives with whom they could discuss their personal problems. Those who attempted suicide were more than twice as likely to report that they had no one to count on compared to a nonsuicidal group.

Homosexuality

In a national 2001 American study, researchers found that gay and bisexual teens were more than twice as likely to be suicidal as their straight counterparts. Fifteen percent of teens with an attraction toward the same sex had considered or attempted suicide, compared to 7 percent of heterosexual teens. Several researchers have suggested that youths who are bisexual or uncertain of their sexual orientation may be at an even higher risk for suicidal behavior than homosexual teenagers.

Myths and Facts

 All suicidal people fully intend to die.
Fact ➛ It is not necessarily true that all suicidal people truly want to end their lives. Many do so and choose methods that are very lethal, such as guns to the head, but there are those who choose methods, such as pills, that may signal a cry for help. They may want to live but not under the prevailing circumstances.

 Friends should not tell on a friend who is talking about suicide. Fact ➛ It is difficult to betray a friend's trust, and you may feel he or she is going to be angry with you, but by telling a responsible adult, you may in fact be saving your friend's life. This is one secret you should not keep!

 People who talk about suicide will not attempt it.
Fact ➛ People who talk about suicide do quite often attempt and even complete suicide. If a teenager mentions that he or she is thinking of suicide, do not brush or laugh it off; take the threat

very seriously. Eighty percent of people give many clues to the fact that they are going to attempt to take their own lives. This means that if you know ten people who constantly talk about suicide, eight of those ten may try it, so take it seriously.

Suicide is hereditary. Fact ➡ Some families do have a history of suicide. Suicidal behavior is not necessarily predetermined genetically, but there is a major concern that once a suicide does exist in a family, other members may be at high risk. People bereaved by suicide, especially family members, are eight times more likely to take their own lives themselves. What is hereditary is a pre-disposition for depression, which can lead to suicidal thoughts.

People who survive a suicide attempt never try again. Fact ➡ Half of all teens who have made one suicide attempt will make another, sometimes as many as two a year until they complete it. In fact, three months after the first attempt, repeat attempts have been noted to occur, even when it looks like the person may be improving. The issues and the problems that led to the suicide attempt need to be altered or changed, otherwise the person may likely try again.

four

HOW DO YOU COPE WITH SUICIDAL THOUGHTS?

If you feel like you would be rejected if people found out about your suicidal thoughts, you're not alone in your thinking. Suicidal teens often hide their true feelings. Many times, the teen feels that he or she has nowhere to go. The pain is unbearable, and he or she sees suicide as a choice. If you are contemplating suicide, you should seek help for your agony. You are not alone, and there are many places you can turn. Here are some places where you can seek help before you take any further negative actions.

Call a Hotline

Call a distress hotline. All conversations are confidential. These lines are manned by specially trained people to give you immediate support and can be helpful for you when you are in crisis. The people who man the hotlines

There are twenty-four-hour hotlines dedicated to helping those who have suicidal thoughts. Take advantage of these services if you ever find yourself thinking about suicide.

are trained to listen to you. They have discussions with you and learn about your problems and feelings of isolation. You can call back at any time if you feel suicidal or just need a helpful voice on the other end. They have had success in doing these immediate crisis interventions. If you ever feel you are in immediate danger, call 911 right away or go directly to your local hospital emergency department.

Turn to People Already in Your Life

Start at home with a parent or guardian, a friend's parent, or your clergy. If that's not working, see a guidance counselor or a coach. Talking to people you trust can also help support you. If you have a teacher whom you highly respect, tell him or her about your suicidal thoughts, even though it may be difficult. Take the risk. In most cases, asking for help is enough to get you the help you need.

Get Professional Help

Make an appointment to see the school social worker, counselor, or psychologist, as these professionals are trained in suicide interventions. Certain hospitals have clinics for teens dealing with depression and suicide. You will need to look in the telephone book or on the Internet to see what clinics are in your hometown. Crisis centers are also places that a teen might feel comfortable seeking help. At crisis centers, teen volunteers or peer counselors use their own experiences and at a teenage level. Talking with them could possibly lead you to get counseling.

Counseling tries to get you to help yourself go from one stage to another to lead a life without pain and sadness as the main focus. A counselor may assess your risk of being suicidal. When you talk to a counselor, he or she will try to understand your sources of stress and your coping mechanisms. A counselor will look for any suicidal warning signs that you may be exhibiting, and if it's determined that you are at risk, your counselor then can offer interventions to support you. All suicide signs are taken very seriously. If you have a suicide plan, be open and share it with your counselor. Also, he or she will need to know if you have attempted suicide before. With a counselor's support, he or she will help you manage your stress and help monitor you so that you have somewhere to go if you are starting to feel that you are spiraling out of control. There are many types of counselors and treatments. You may need to shop around to get the person that best meshes with your personality.

Handling Stress

It is important for you to understand that you cannot eliminate stress entirely from your life, but you can learn how to manage it and reduce some of the distress it causes. You may not be able to control things, but you can control your reactions to those things. More positive ways to handle stress are through activities such as talking to someone who cares, exercising, listening to or playing music, and spending time with friends.

Though you may feel that spending time with friends is out of the question because of schoolwork and family obligations, it's an important stress reliever.

Treatment

If someone were to ask you right now, at this present moment, if you are having thoughts of suicide, what would your answer be? If the answer is "maybe" or "yes," then this is a really difficult time for you. There is no reason to go through this time alone. If you're feeling depressed and are thinking of suicide, you should seek help. There are many types of treatments out there, and you might have to experiment with a few kinds before you find one that is suitable for you. You also need to find a therapist whom you feel that you can work with. One method of treatment might not be the answer. A combination of treatments might be more useful.

Getting Treatment

The first step for you to find the right treatment is to go to your family members or someone you trust to see who or what organization they can recommend. The school guidance counselor, social worker, and psychologist are all people whom you should feel safe in asking for support. You can also contact your family doctor to ask him or her to help refer you to an appropriate therapist. The local hospital is also a place to start to see if it has groups that may be beneficial to you. The important first step is to say to yourself that you do not need to go through life all by yourself feeling this way. There are those out there to help you, so please seek the help.

There are many different kinds of treatments. The specialist you go to will probably favor one treatment over the other. The goal of all treatments is to try and get you to function day to day without thinking of suicide as an option.

Group Treatment

You may find group therapy helpful because other teens are present. At group therapy, you can talk about the things in your life that cause stress and you might find somebody in the group who can relate with you.

Brief Crisis-Oriented Treatment

Schools often have this type of treatment, and it's best for depressed people who are not diagnosed as clinically depressed and do not have drug and alcohol abuse problems. Sessions might be oriented toward problem solving, might require that your parents attend, and might include activities such as role playing. Crisis-oriented treatment involves five interrelated stages: assessment, problem solving, preventive measures, termination, and follow-up.

Peer Counseling

When high school students were given a choice of whom they would first confide in if they were having suicidal thoughts, 91 percent reported that they would confide in a friend before going to a parent, teacher, or other adult, according to the Board of Education for the City of Hamilton (Ontario, Canada). The percentage was considerably lower for teens that said they would not confide in anyone. If teens are going to confide in anyone, their first choice appears to be a peer.

For this reason, a number of schools have developed peer counseling programs. You will need to go to the school guidance office and ask if there is peer counseling available to you. Much of what peer counselors teach is interpersonal and social problem-solving skills, and they can serve as a bridge between you and professionals. Once you are seeing your own professional therapist, you may still need the support from both groups but may choose to go only to your therapist. If you're contemplating suicide, peer counselors will refer you to a professional, somebody who is trained to handle crises. They are instructed to refer you to an adult if you report that you are feeling suicidal.

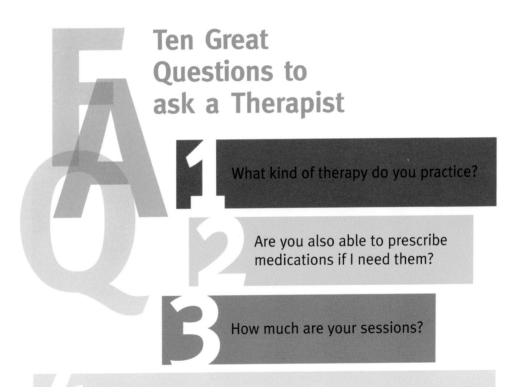

Ten Great Questions to ask a Therapist

1 What kind of therapy do you practice?

2 Are you also able to prescribe medications if I need them?

3 How much are your sessions?

4 What is the process of therapy, and what are the goals? How do you see me achieving them?

5 Do you think it is a good idea to keep a journal of my thoughts?

6 What happens if I feel uncomfortable in the sessions?

7 Are our sessions confidential?
Will you tell my parents what I say?

8 Will you also be seeing other members of my family or peer group?

9 What will you do if I say I am feeling suicidal or I am having suicidal thoughts?

10 Do you have any good resources that you can recommend to me?

five

HOW DO YOU GET THERAPY?

To get a therapist, you usually need a referral. Your family doctor can give you one. There can be a cost for some therapists. This must be discussed with your family. Some therapists have sliding scales, and some are connected to agencies that may help you in your time of crisis. Your parents might also have a drug or health plan that will cover the cost of your treatment.

What Is Therapy?

Psychotherapy comes in many forms. In general, psychotherapy is a process in which a patient talks with a mental health professional about problems, such as relationships, emotional issues, or mental health conditions. The psychotherapist, a person with specialized training in treating these conditions, uses

If you're feeling depressed for long periods of time for no apparent reason, you may have clinical depression. If this is the case, it's important to talk to a professional.

various techniques, including reassurance, insight, persuasion, and information, to help patients (or clients) see themselves and their problems in new and different ways so that they can deal with them more effectively.

Psychotherapy is based on a therapeutic relationship between the therapist and the patient. The person who chooses a therapist is usually called a patient because the therapist is often, though not always, a person in the medical (or related) field.

Does talking about problems really help? The answer is yes, it does. No one knows exactly why this happens, but have you noticed that when you talk about something that's bothering you, you feel better afterward? Most often, you probably talk to a close friend or family member about problems or the things on your mind. But sometimes that's not enough. You may need more intense help or a more objective person to talk to.

At times, everyone feels alone, confused, or "stuck." It's part of the human condition. But you don't have to feel that way all the time. Help is available. The decision to reach out to a professional for support and guidance can be one of the best and most important decisions of your life.

What Can Therapy Do?

Psychological therapy (as opposed to physical therapy or occupational therapy, for example) is based on the premise that change comes from awareness (sometimes called insight). Through a trusting relationship with a therapist, you will get the courage to take a sometimes scary look at yourself. You may begin to understand why you do things you don't even like in spite of your best efforts not to do them. You will be able to drop these sometimes negative, self-destructive, and even dangerous behaviors and act differently.

It is important to remember that therapy is based on a relationship with a person who has expertise in treating people with problems. Often when your behavior seems out of control to yourself and others, there is a hidden agenda that even you don't understand. For example, cracking jokes during a teacher's lecture may get you some attention but not the kind of attention you're looking for. A therapist can help you discover what you really want from life.

Confidentiality

As you think about therapy, it is important to understand confidentiality. Confidentiality means that your therapist will keep your trust by not revealing to anyone the matters you discuss in your sessions. This is especially true if you are of legal age. There are exceptions, however, and they include:

- Suicide threats
- Threats of self-injury
- Threats to kill others or harm them
- Disclosing any kind of abuse
- Intent to commit a crime
- Psychosis (loss of touch with reality)
- Court-ordered evaluations

You are probably most concerned about what the therapist might tell your parents. Many states extend confidentiality to persons under eighteen years of age. Your therapist will probably explain this to you when you initially meet. If a therapist believes that something you have said is important for your parents to know, he or she will probably try to help you find a way to tell them yourself.

Why Consider Therapy?

Let's be honest. Therapy may not be your idea. In fact, there is probably a very good chance that it isn't your idea. Not only that, but you don't want to go.

Sometimes, a judge orders an individual into therapy. More often, the suggestion that you might benefit from seeing a therapist comes from your parents, a teacher, or a school counselor—and that can be one reason why you don't want to do it.

But before digging in your heels, give the concept a chance and get into the planning. You're the person who will benefit. Do you want someone else choosing your therapist?

Some people have described therapists as "paid friends." Well, why not hire a trained professional to help you deal with such important matters as thoughts, feelings, and problems? If you had pneumonia, you would try to find the best physician available to treat it.

You do pay people to do other things for you—to cut your hair, to fix your car, to serve you food at a restaurant. Are your thoughts, feelings, and problems worth less attention than your hair, your car, or your taste buds?

Remember that psychotherapy is based on a therapeutic relationship with a person who has training and expertise in treating people with problems. Therapists work in different ways to help you accomplish your goals. But the therapist can't do all the work. Making changes in your behavior isn't easy; it requires patience and will take some effort on your part.

You shouldn't feel ashamed about going to counseling or therapy. They are important, and sometimes lifesaving, treatments for serious depression.

Is Counseling the Same as Psychotherapy?

What's the difference between counseling and psychotherapy? Some people use these terms interchangeably. If you're embarrassed about seeing a professional to help solve personal problems, it may seem easier to say, "I'm going to talk to my counselor," than to say, "I'm going to my psychotherapist."

The term "counselor" often refers to someone who gives advice about short-term practical matters such as study habits, courses, jobs, or future professions. Some counselors also teach—about problems such as drug or alcohol abuse. Counseling tends to be more informal and short-term, maybe one to five sessions.

Psychotherapy (or therapy) is usually for more intense, long-term problems, such as anxiety, depression, low self-esteem, substance abuse, or eating disorders. Previous efforts you've made on your own to take control of these problems haven't worked. For example:

⇒ You eat so little your bones are showing and your clothes don't fit
⇒ You do things you don't want to do, such as stealing
⇒ You drink alcohol from bottles you hide in your bedroom

What Therapy Can't Do

Although we compared therapy to getting a haircut, your therapist is not your haircutter. And as good as a massage feels, your massage-giver is not your therapist. Therapy is not getting and giving advice, although advice may be a part of it. Therapy is not about getting the therapist to like you. Therapy is not about feeling comfortable. (In fact, therapy may make you feel uncomfortable—at least for a time.)

Family Therapy

In family therapy, the therapist may see individuals alone or the family as a whole. Family therapy is supportive not only for teens but for other members of the family who may be experiencing difficulties in relating to each other. Some of the goals of family therapy are:

Family therapy is an alternative to one-on-one therapy, especially if you feel that your family dynamics are the root of your depression and suicidal thoughts.

➤ Get you to see your place in the family
➤ Get you to see the family dynamics and make positive changes
➤ Get your parents to understand the seriousness of the suicidal threat or attempt
➤ Get the whole family to work together in an appropriate and supportive manner to help you
➤ Get your family to understand their conflicts and how to solve them among themselves

Some people find family therapy beneficial because members of the family can work together to address concerns and heal together.

Psychodynamic Psychotherapy

This form of therapy encourages the exploration of conscious and unconscious emotional issues to help you understand and deal with emotional responses to conflictful relationships. You may find yourself in repeated patterns of relating to others that are not working. When these patterns cause emotional turmoil, psychodynamic therapy can help you make significant changes in how you see and interact with your world. Long-term psychiatric treatment enables a patient-therapist bond to develop.

Since suicide is not usually an impulse decision, many see that longer therapy may be a better method. Long-term psychiatric treatment enables a patient-therapist bond to develop. A trained therapist could then help you sort out your anger and conscious and unconscious behavior, and help provide strategies for you to deal with them successfully.

Cognitive Behavioral Therapy

In cognitive behavioral therapy, the therapist focuses on your cognition. Cognition is the way in which you see your own reality and interpret your world. Many suicidal teens have three negative views:

1. A negative view of themselves
2. A negative view of the world
3. A negative view of the future or a sense of hopelessness

The therapist helps you see your world in a more positive light. The sessions usually last about twelve weeks, approximately twenty sessions or more.

Psychopharmacological Therapy

When a doctor feels that you have a tendency toward depression, medication may be prescribed. Unfortunately, there is no "anti-suicide" pill that can be given to make you all better. There are antidepressant medications to stabilize your mood and relieve your symptoms, and there are other medications to control accompanying anxiety and excessive eating and sleeping. It appears that medication alone is not the sole answer in supporting you if you are feeling suicidal. You will probably need a combination of medication and talk therapy. Many drugs do have side effects, and so you'll need to be closely monitored. Since you could still be at a high risk for suicide, the access to the pills must be severely limited.

Hospitalization

When depression is severe enough, or a suicide has been attempted, you might require hospitalization. This may entail confinement in the psychiatric ward of a hospital and placing all staff on high alert and putting you on suicide watch. Although hospitalization may seem scary, it is a time in which specialists can help direct the next steps in preventing reoccurrence, like assessing for drug and alcohol abuse and understanding the risk factors. This is also a time that you may be treated with medications like antidepressants or antianxiety drugs as well as making sure you have somebody to go to for counseling when you leave the hospital.

six

IS YOUR LOVED ONE SUICIDAL?

Young people who have attempted suicide exhibit classic warning signs. When people talk about suicide, listen, as it can be a cry for help.

Warning Signs

If your friend starts making comments like he or she soon will not be hurting anymore, people will be sorry when he or she is gone, and everyone would be better off without him or her, you should be concerned. Some other worrying signs are when your friend starts asking more information about dying, such as whether you think dying hurts. He or she may indicate that he or she wants the sadness and depression to go away and may want to do something about it. These are cries for help, and they must be heard.

Warning signs such as listening to hateful, angry music should be taken seriously, both by yourself and by peers.

Some other signs that need immediate response include constantly talking about death, asking about different ways to take his or her own life (learning the amount of a lethal dose of medication, how to get a gun, etc.), and actually saying he or she wants to kill him- or herself. Your friend may be preoccupied with books and music that have the common theme of suicide or be busy planning his or her own funeral. Obvious signs are when a person starts putting affairs in order, making any final wishes known to friends and family, and giving away personal belongings.

What You Can Do

Do not leave a suicidal person alone. Call a responsible member of the family, a crisis help line, or if necessary, 911. You could save a life.

When someone is thinking of suicide, try and encourage him or her to talk to a person who is trusted, such as a parent, a guardian, or a teacher. Maybe your friend needs to talk to a guidance counselor, social worker, someone in the mental health profession, or a member of his or her clergy.

It is important to be a good friend and listen. Always take your friend seriously, and do not make jokes about his or her feelings. Be interested in your friend's emotions and actions. Remember to remain calm and be nonjudgmental, and offer appropriate options. Don't say:

- Don't worry, things will get better in time.
- You should not feel that way.

If you think your friend is at risk, get rid of any accessible guns, pills, ropes, or anything else that could cause harm. Be there to offer any help or assistance. If it becomes over your head and the situation is turning into a crisis, tell a trusted adult. Remember, do not be sworn to secrecy. Seek help.

After a Loved One Completes Suicide

Once a teen has completed suicide, many people are affected. The devastated family and friends are known as "survivors."

What many young people fail to realize is that there are many victims of individual suicides, including friends, family, and other loved ones.

There are millions of survivors each year trying to deal with the loss of their loved ones who died from suicide. Suicide survivors suffer in three ways: first, because they are grieving for the deceased; second, because they are suffering from the traumatic experience; and third, because people do not talk about suicide. Therefore, it is difficult to confide in your closest friends and family members and receive the response you may have received if it was another kind of death.

Coping Within Your Family

If you have a sibling who completed suicide, you are a very vulnerable survivor. You must struggle with your own grief, as well as guilt, anger, sadness, and other strong emotions. Unfortunately, your parents are also dealing with their own grief, and they may feel unfit as parents. They might want to give you the attention that you need but may not feel they have the strength to do it. You may start feeling neglected and troubled, or you might take on a parental role and view your parents as the children.

You need to be able to heal together as a family. Blaming each other will not help. Talking together and sharing emotions will be better for everyone in the long run. If you have younger siblings in your family, they may not understand the reactions around them. They may feel the death is their fault, or they may feel abandoned by their loved one. They, too, may benefit from children-oriented therapy, like play or art therapy.

Ways to Cope

The following are ways that may help you in your despair. Anniversaries, holidays, and birthdays may be difficult. You may feel intense sadness in the days leading up to these special events. You may want to create a ritual, like making a special card in honor of the loved one or visiting the grave and placing flowers on it. (Some people find going to the graveyard too depressing whereas others find it a refuge.)

Suicidal thoughts and depression don't necessarily need to be treated by psychotherapy. Physical activities can greatly improve your outlook on life.

It is really important that you take care of your own personal well-being. You should eat right, exercise, and try to get enough sleep. This is not the time to take up risky behaviors like smoking, drinking, drugs, and sex just to drown out or not look at your feelings.

You may need to go to a bereavement group or see a social worker, psychologist, psychiatrist, school guidance counselor, clergy person, or any professional person whom you feel comfortable enough to talk to and who you feel can guide you through the therapeutic experience. There are also crisis intervention hotlines and centers that are staffed by trained personnel who offer guidance and support.

The tragic fact about suicide is that it is permanent. There is no bringing back to life the person who has completed suicide. What can you do? Be aware of the warning signs. If you know a person who feels all alone, take a moment and find out why. If you see people who are depressed, take a moment to help get assistance for them. If you see people who are crying out for help, recognize their pain and help support them. Do not keep suicide under lock and key. Make a difference to another young life by offering your hand. If you are feeling suicidal yourself, seek help. Please take the hand that is being offered.

Glossary

assessment An evaluation, usually performed by a physician, of a person's mental, emotional, and social capabilities.

autocide A suicide that is disguised as or appears to be an automobile accident.

bisexual Having sexual attraction to both males and females.

chronic Lasting a long period of time.

clinical depression A state of depression so severe as to require treatment.

cluster suicides Two or more teen suicides that happen around the same time or in the same way; also called copycat suicides.

correlated Describes complementary relationship between things.

depression The condition of feeling sad and despondent.

harass To irritate, torment.

heterosexual Being sexually attracted to people of the opposite sex.

hotline A call center where professionals trained to help with a problem answer phone lines.

pessimism A tendency to view the negative.

prevalent Commonly occurring.

ritual A ceremonial act.

suicide The act of intentionally taking one's own life.

suicide rate The percentage of people in a specific group who take their own lives in a certain duration of time.

warning signs Specific observable behaviors, actions, and circumstances of an individual in crisis. These symptoms may indicate that the individual is at risk of suicide.

American Association of Suicidology
4201 Connecticut Avenue NW, Suite 408
Washington, DC 20008
(202) 237-2280
Web site: http://www.suicidology.org
   This national organization seeks to educate and train
   suicide prevention professionals to end the occurrence
   of suicide.

American Foundation for Suicide Prevention
120 Wall Street, 22nd Floor
New York, NY 10005
(888) 333-AFSP (2377)
Web site: http://www.afsp.org
   This national nonprofit organization provides research
   and outreach for people who may be at risk for suicide.

HealthyPlace.com
Web site: http://www.healthyplace.com
   A Web site providing mental health information, support,
   and the opportunity to share experiences helpful to others.

National Alliance on Mental Illness (NAMI)
2107 Wilson Boulevard, Suite 300

Arlington, VA 22201-3042

(800) 950-NAMI (6264)

Web site: http://www.nami.org

NAMI is the nation's largest grassroots mental health organization dedicated to improving the lives of persons living with
serious mental illness.

National Foundation for Depressive Illness, Inc.

P.O. Box 2257

New York, NY 10116

(800) 248-4344

Web site: http://www.depression.org

A good resource for information on depression. The Web site
also offers links to most of the major associations dealing with
depression.

National Mental Health Association (NMHA)

2000 N. Beauregard Street, 6th Floor

Alexandria, VA 22311

(703) 684-7722

Web site: http://www.nmha.org

The NMHA is the country's oldest and largest nonprofit
organization addressing all aspects of mental health and
mental illness.

Suicide Awareness Voices of Education (SAVE)

9001 East Bloomington Freeway, Suite 150

Bloomington, MN 55420

(952) 946-7998

Web site: http://www.save.org

   This nonprofit group is mainly composed of survivors of suicide.

Web Sites

Due to the changing nature of Internet links, Rosen Publishing
has developed an online list of Web sites related to the subject
of this book. This site is updated regularly. Please use this link
to access the list:

http://www.rosenlinks.com/faq/suic

Berman, Alan L., David A. Jobes, and Morton M. Silverman. *Adolescent Suicide: Assessment and Intervention*. 2nd ed. Washington, DC: American Psychological Association, 2005.

Blauner, Susan Rose. *How I Stayed Alive When My Brain Was Trying to Kill Me*. New York, NY: HarperCollins, 2003.

Box, Matthew J. *Suicide*. San Diego, CA: Greenhaven Press, 2005.

Crook, Marion. *Teens Talk About Suicide*. Vancouver, Canada: Arsenal Pulp Press, 2004.

Elkind, David. *The Hurried Child: Growing Up Too Fast and Too Soon*. New York, NY: Basic Books, 2001.

Empfield, Maureen, and Nick Bakalar. *Understanding Teenage Depression: A Guide to Diagnosis, Treatment, and Management*. New York, NY: Henry Holt and Company, 2001.

Levac, Anne Marie. *Helping Your Teenager Beat Depression: A Problem-Solving Approach for Families*. Bethesda, MD: Woodbine House, 2004.

Marr, Neil, and Tom Field. *Bullycide Death at Playtime*. Oxfordshire, England: Success Unlimited, 2000.

Murphy, James. *Coping with Teen Suicide*. New York, NY: Rosen Publishing, 1999.

Peacock, Judith. *Teen Suicide*. Minneapolis, MN: Compass Point Books, 2005.

Roleff, Tamara L. *Teen Suicide*. San Diego, CA: Greenhaven Press, 2000.

Sperekas, Nicole B. *SuicideWise: Taking Steps Against Teen Suicide*. Berkeley Heights, NJ: Enslow Publishers, 2000.

Wallerstein, Claire. *Teen Suicide*. Chicago, IL: Heinemann Library, 2003.

Index

About the Author

Sandra Giddens is a special education consultant at the Toronto District School Board. She has her doctorate in education and has written a number of books for Rosen Publishing.

Photo Credits

Cover © Myrleen Ferguson/Photo Edit; p. 5 © www.istockphoto.com/ Saatu Knape; p. 6 © WireImage/Getty Images; p. 8 © Amy Etra/Photo Edit; p. 11 © Richard Heinzen/SuperStock; p. 14 © Bob Daemmrich/ The Image Works; p. 16 © Getty Images; p. 18 © Ellen Senisi/The Image Works; p. 21 © www.istockphoto.com/Jason Stitt; p. 23 © National Geographic/Getty Images; p. 24 © Mary Kate Denny/Photo Edit; p. 29 © Geri Engberg/The Image Works; p. 32 © www.istockphoto. com/Abimelec Olan; p. 38 © Sean O'Brien/Custom Medical Stock Photo; p. 42 © www.istockphoto.com; p. 44 © Jonathan Nourok; Photo Edit; p. 49 © Shutterstock; p. 51© Peter Byron/Photo Edit; p. 53 © www.istockphoto.com/Jason Stephens.

Designer: Evelyn Horovicz; Editor: Nicholas Croce
Photo Researcher: Marty Levick